EFFECTIVE IMMEDIATELY... I QUIT

WHY GOOD EMPLOYEES LEAVE

by Jamaevra Jackson

DORRANCE
PUBLISHING CO
EST. 1920
PITTSBURGH, PENNSYLVANIA 15238

Dorrance Publishing Co
585 Alpha Drive
Pittsburgh, PA 15238
Visit our website at *www.dorrancebookstore.com*

ISBN: 979-8-8860-4319-8
eISBN: 979-8-8860-4588-8

INTRODUCTION

Good employees leave jobs all the time. Often the circumstances leading to their resignations are not ideal, but they are rarely able to provide true explanations. After leaving, stories are created to make former employees seem incompetent or simply smear their reputations, and they are unable to defend themselves. When interviewing for other positions, good employees regularly fabricate reasons for leaving that are "more professional" and doesn't make them sound like they are complaining. No matter how much research backs up the negativity in workplaces, our society does not want to hear the truth.

For years, I went to work every day and came home miserable every night. No matter how hard I tried to mind my business and do a good job, work did not get better. It would actually get worse. So I would find another job and repeat the cycle. I tried different ways to manage stress at work and at home. Meditation, exercise, crafts, coloring, writing in journals, gaming, and of course, drinking. Nothing helped until the day where I finally had enough and quit. I decided that if I have to constantly be ready for a battle at work, then I should not be there. It would be different if I were in the military, but I worked in office buildings.

This book focuses on reasons why employees leave their jobs and uses my personal experiences as the basis and not scientific research. I have nothing against scientific research, and I think it is very important, but I wanted to share my personal experiences in hopes that I can encourage someone else and let them know that they are not alone and that better opportunities do exist. They just have to be willing to find them.

CHAPTER 1
INCOMPETENT LEADERSHIP

"Good employees don't quit jobs, they quit bad bosses." This is a saying that's repeated often and is posted on social media practically every day. Apparently, the concept seems to be common knowledge that is well understood by many individuals across diverse backgrounds. So why is it still an issue in most organizations? Specifically, organizations who find themselves regularly managing high attrition rates. As I made the decision to move into a career in human resources, I slowly realized an alarming fact. Incompetent leadership is tolerated by those in authority because it does not pose a threat to them. You may disagree with me if you would like, that comes with the territory, but think about it. How many times have you had jobs that you complained that your manager or direct supervisor did not know what they were doing? They have a track record of mismanaging employees, having employees complete their own performance evaluations, developing work schedules that leaves the organization understaffed during peak times, giving incorrect information, coming in late, leaving early, overspending the budget, or being just plain stupid, BUT they still come to work and collect a paycheck. So what's really going on? They are not a threat to someone else.

I once had a supervisor who would go out of her way to sound smart and used words incorrectly in the process. After annual performance appraisals, I received an email from her explaining that I was eligible for the merit increase that year. The email went a little something like this.

"Jamaevra - In lieu of your hard work, you will be receiving a merit increase of 2.5%."

Do you see the problem with this statement? First, the phrase "in lieu of" means to replace or substitute. So, if I were to interpret the meaning of this statement the way it was written I could have concluded that she was saying, "Jamaevra – Instead of your hard work, you will be receiving a merit increase of 2.5%." But I didn't take this as the meaning because it makes no logical sense. Unfortunately, for me to know what she was trying to tell me, I had to lower my level of intelligence. Now the rest of the statement was also a disappointment, but I will get into that later.

There were other instances with this manager that made me question her abilities. One of my job tasks was to track planned absences, unplanned absences, and absences relating to FMLA in a monthly attendance report. Management wanted me to begin breaking down the FMLA portion based on reason. Now if you know anything about FMLA law or HR, you would know that the reasons for qualified leave under FMLA are confidential.

HR TIP: If you are requesting leave covered under FMLA, the only people who should know the full details of your leave are you and your healthcare provider. When the healthcare provider completes their portion of the FMLA request form and provides supporting documentation, the limited information that is provided is HIPAA (Health Insurance Portability and Accountability Act) compliant and should only be used to help HR determine if the requested leave is a qualifying reason under FMLA. From there, HR should only inform the supervisor if the FMLA request is approved or denied. To protect employee privacy, supervisors should not be provided full details regarding the reasons for FMLA requests. You, the employee, may disclose more details to your supervisor if you choose but it is not required. Any unauthorized disclosure of your healthcare information by your employer or supervisor is a violation of your rights and you should file an official compliant or grievance following the process outlined in your employee handbook.

Now back to the story.

So when I received this request, my response was, "I can provide you the number of individuals who were on FMLA at any given time. However, I will be unable to provide details regarding reasons for FMLA because I do not have access to this information." Another thing you should know is I was NOT a member of the human resources department and did not have any direct reports. At the time, I was a regular line staff member. The response I received basically accused me of refusing work or insubordination. Me being the person I am, I emailed the original request, my response, and my supervisor's response to our Human Resources Department and HR said...

"For the purposes of your position, you do not have nor will you gain access to detailed information relating to FMLA absences. This information is restricted to the employee, the employee's direct supervisor, the supervisor's manager (if necessary), and the human resources department. Please have your supervisor reach out to us with any additional questions."

I forwarded this response from HR to my supervisor and cc'd her supervisor. That should have been the end of it, right? Nope, it wasn't. Then my supervisor came to me and said, "What do you hear about people who are on FMLA?" My response, "I don't hear anything. I only need to know if they are here or not for the purposes of doing my job. Anything beyond that is irrelevant to me." Then she goes "Well, the only reasons people would be on FMLA is for maternity leave, right?" I had no response, just a confused stare. What do you say to that? I was thinking, "Yeah, the employee who is a man in his late 50's is out of the office because he gave birth." All I could think was, "This is the person who is responsible for my performance evaluation." Sadness.

So I told her, "Look, I can develop a report based on the data that I'm authorized to have but I will not create something that's based on speculation or gossip." Was I wrong? Some would say "yes" because she was my supervisor and she instructed me to complete a task. But people who have some level of integrity would say no. My reason: when I do my job, I do it to the best of my abilities and I expect quality. If anything jeopardizes the expectations I have set for myself, I will not touch it. Period. I believe in doing things right or not at all. Half-assing is a practice that is too widely accepted.

Anywho, these are just a couple of examples from one incompetent "leader" that I have encountered in my professional life thus far. There is so much more that I can share but this chapter would be WAY too long. So, let's move on.

Now I can't speak for everyone, but incompetent leadership is difficult for me to deal with. Everyone has to answer to someone, and I get that. But when I accept a position, I expect my supervisor to be somewhat knowledgeable about the business unit that they oversee. Additionally, if I have already been in a position and a new person is hired that I'm supposed to report to, I expect them to be fully competent. Especially if I were passed over for the promotion. To me, this means that the person who was ultimately hired should be more qualified and experienced than I am. So what happens when talented workers are passed over for promotions and expected to train their new supervisor? I tell you what, the clock starts ticking until they walk out the door for good.

When I have been faced with this type of situation, I felt like the managers in my area were telling me, "You're good enough to do the work but we aren't going to pay you for it." I can admit, there were times when this has happened, and I would try to help my new supervisor as much as I could. But they eventually started expecting me to tell them everything they needed to know and when I didn't, I was suddenly difficult or insubordinate. For years, going with the flow and doing what I had to do was out of necessity. I have been a single parent since I was 18 and I have two kids who rely on me. So do I knowingly put myself in a situation where I could lose my job or do I shut my mouth and do as I was told? This was always my dilemma, but I've always seemed to approach it a little differently than most.

First, I believe that when God gives you a job, no matter what company provides your paycheck, you work for Him. I believe God places us in situations to see how we will handle them before He blesses us with more. If you prove to God that you can't be trusted with a little, why should you expect to have more? You can't have a million-dollar dream on a minimum wage work ethic. I believe that when you have a job, you are supposed to do it to the best of your abilities. If you don't, I think you are hindering your future blessings. This belief also causes me to place that same expectation on those who I report to. We have built a society that allows mediocre people to ascend to high positions because of who they know and not what they know. Just as I am expected to have constant exemplary performance in my job, I expect the same of anyone in a supervisory/managerial role. And I'm not afraid to show it.

Incompetent leaders may not know much about their actual jobs or the jobs of the people who report to them, but they all know how to exercise their authority. So when an incompetent supervisor begins to throw their weight around, it's in your best interest to know your rights as well. I have been threatened with write-ups and termination, and I've responded, "You do whatever you feel is necessary and I will do the same." If I had low performance, their threats would have carried some weight. So if I have to go down, I'm going down fighting. There have been a few instances where I didn't care enough to fight and I just quit. In recent years, I have realized, if I have to go to war at work every day, then I shouldn't be there. Especially since I know the current job is not my ultimate goal or the best I can do. I may give you a two-week notice but then again, I may not. Depends on how I feel about you and how I have been treated during my time of employment. Reporting to someone who is incompetent is emotionally and mentally draining, because you are constantly on edge, which is stressful. At the time of writing this book, I am 38 years old. I'm young but old enough to know what I deserve. The older I get, the less understanding and patient I am with foolishness, and I try to choose my battles wisely.

CHAPTER 2

UNWILLING TO KISS ASS

There are many, many talented workers in this world with diverse educational backgrounds and experience levels. I am always amazed about what humans are able to accomplish when they put forth the effort. But no matter how many skills and abilities talented workers have, the one ability none of them possess is "ass-kissing" and it will forever remain an undeveloped skill. When a person is confident in their abilities, they have no reason to brown-nose, kiss-up, kiss ass, or whatever you want to call it. Employees who are willing to stroke the egos of their boss only do so because they are insecure with their abilities. Unfortunately, when you report to a manager who is incompetent, they will always show favoritism to employees who make them feel important, no matter how bad that employee is at performing their actual duties. If you don't believe me, just observe your co-workers. The people who produce the least and make the most mistakes will be the best brown-nosers and be treated very well.

June 2005 to January 2006, I had a position where I scheduled medical appointments for Nephrology and Pulmonary clinics and was backup for Cardiology, Rheumatology, Infectious Disease, and Allergy clinics. There may have been more, but that's what I remember.

Patients would call and I would schedule or reschedule their appointments. Calls came in all day, and in between calls, we would make outbound reminder calls to patients. Not the most interesting job, but it's an important one. One day the supervisor came in and just about all of my co-workers set their phones not to accept calls and began talking to her. When one person sets their phone not to receive calls, the calls just continue rolling to other employees who are available. As I was one of the few who did not turn off their phone, my calls kept rolling with no break. When she got around to me, she spoke and asked how I was doing, I muted my phone and said, "Hello, I'm good. How are you?" By then, I needed to respond to the patient that I was also on the phone with and resumed working. My supervisor went into the hallway and said to one of my coworkers, "I never would have hired her if I knew she had such a bad attitude." What the hell? How did me putting the patient/customer first and continuing to do the job I was paid to do equate to me having a bad attitude? Then she added drama to it by making the statement to my co-worker, which is a separate problem.

Now, I assume the visit was just to check on staff, which was a good thing, but the way it was done was disruptive and inappropriate. Her visit couldn't have been more than ten minutes, but the issue isn't what she did, but HOW she did it. Our team was divided into two offices. One office was about 20' x 10' with five people, and the office I was in was maybe 8' x 10' with three people in it. Because we worked in very close quarters, side conversations were disruptive to our calls. But I guess that was not important. It seemed to be more important to her for the staff to acknowledge her and make her feel important.

As a manager, you should understand the jobs of your employees as well as their work conditions. Understanding these two factors will help you create effective interactions that do not negatively impact workflow. If she just wanted to check on us individually, there were other ways to accomplish this goal without being disruptive.

OPTION #1 — Send an email. While we would have lacked the face-to-face interaction, an email could have been sent. A simple message saying something like, "Hi, I'm just checking in to see how things are going. If you need anything, let me know. My door is always open. Thanks for all you do" would have been effective and not disruptive.

OPTION #2 — One-on-One meetings. She could have scheduled times for each staff member to meet with her in private. This time allows workflow to continue while improving the employee/supervisor relationship in a private face-to-face interaction.

Needless to say, this was a position that I eventually left. Honestly, I just stopped caring. I rarely came to work on time and my unplanned absences increased, but I still produced quality work [when I showed up]. Subconsciously, I think I wanted to get fired but it didn't happen, and I ended up resigning after six about months of employment.

CHAPTER 3

INCOMPETENT COWORKERS

Working with incompetent coworkers can be more of a headache than having an incompetent supervisor. Especially if you are good at your job. In many cases, the mistakes made by underperforming employees is redirected to employees who have good performance. From a supervisor's perspective, this approach is taken because it's just easier. You know which employees you can trust to get the job done without you looking over their shoulder. Honestly, it's less stressful on the supervisor to just reassign the work. But many supervisors don't think about the other side(s) of this situation.

From the perspective of the high performer – While it is a good feeling to know that your manager trusts you and is confident in your abilities, it is not a good feeling to be taken for granted. As time passes, high performers unintentionally acquire higher workloads than their coworkers who have less than ideal performance. As their stress levels increase, their morale can decrease. If the workload continues to rise, you may begin to notice a decrease in performance, a change in attitude, and possibly receive a resignation from the very person who you counted on.

From the perspective of the low performer – Jackpot! They have been successful at reducing their workload while continuing to receive a full paycheck. In my experience, the employees who have the lowest workloads cause the most drama and engage in the most counterproductive activities, i.e. gossiping and surfing the internet. These types of non-work-related activities are not a good use of company resources.

For all the supervisors, there is another way to handle underperforming employees. It's called Training and Development. Unfortunately, training and development will temporarily increase your work. But if you are a supervisor/manager, this falls under your responsibilities no matter what company you work for. If you want the title, then do the job. Instead of reassigning work, try this approach. Be sure to document actions and discussions accordingly.

#1. VALIDATE TRAINING — Many times, underperforming employees make mistakes because they do not know any better. I have had jobs where I have not received training and was left on my own to figure it out. While a few employees may thrive in this type of environment, many do not. As the supervisor, you should ensure that your direct reports have received proper training before punishing them for not meeting performance expectations. But before you can ensure that someone else has been properly trained, you should first make sure you understand the process.

#2. GIVE CONSTRUCTIVE FEEDBACK — Once you have validated that the underperforming employee has been properly trained, you need to keep a close eye on their work. Meet with the employee IN PRIVATE (without being condescending), let them know what was wrong, and explain the desired expectations, which align with business objectives and not your ego. If you don't explain what the expectations are, you are continuing the cycle and will make your life harder. Provide constructive feedback that is honest and timely. As with parenting, it is ineffective to discipline a child two weeks after they engaged in an undesired behavior because they will not know what was wrong. The same principle applies with employee feedback and discipline. You should address the issue while it's fresh in the employee's mind. This allows them to adjust accordingly and work to avoid additional mistakes.

#3. MONITOR PERFORMANCE — You will need to monitor performance and provide feedback (as necessary) for a specified period of time. Depending on the severity of the issue, this can be two weeks or 30 days. You will need to determine a reasonable amount of time for the specific situation. Monitoring performance may include having the employee send their work to you for review before final submission, periodically pulling work samples, or randomly observing their behavior. The method you choose is dependent upon the specific situation. Once the employee has reached the desired performance level, leave them to perform on their own.

#4. RECOGNIZE IMPROVEMENTS — This can be a simple email that says, "Hey, I just wanted to let you know that your performance has improved. Your commitment and efforts are not unnoticed. If you need anything, feel free to reach out. Keep up the great work." Simple and to the point. It doesn't take much to tell someone that they are doing a good job.

Now, if you have validated training, given feedback, monitored performance, and have had to repeat the cycle two or more times, clearly the employee is not understanding the job and may not be a good fit for the position. In this case, do what you have to do (according to company policies and federal/state employment laws) to remove the underperformer and hire a qualified replacement. Allow high performers to assist with the workload in the interim, but only until a suitable replacement has been identified. Remember, there are too many people who are currently seeking jobs and would do a great job for you to settle for someone who is not a good fit. Yes, turnover costs are high, but a bad employee costs even more.

CHAPTER 4

UNCHALLENGING WORK

There are plenty of employees who will jump at the chance to have a job that takes little to no effort and they get to take home a paycheck and receive benefits. But we are not talking about those employees; we are talking about good employees.

In my experience as an employee and supervisor, the best employees enjoy being challenged and often welcome the opportunity to work on special projects because this allows them to enhance their skills to further their career. But when you have an employee who is highly skilled and has a natural drive to do a great job, do yourself a favor and put that talent to good use, but don't overwork them. Let me explain what I mean.

When you manage people, you are expected to delegate work so that your business unit effectively contributes to the achievement of the organization's strategic goals and objectives. When the presence of a high performer is detected, many managers and supervisors get so happy that they tend to forget they have other employees. Whenever anything extra needs to be done, they automatically assign the task to the high performer. At first, the high performing employee is flattered because they know their good work is being noticed and they are trusted by leadership. But overtime, the "honeymoon phase" fades away as they notice their workloads are significantly higher than their peers, and/or they have not received a raise or promotion. From the perspective of the supervisor, they continue to delegate work to the high performers because they can trust them to do the job correctly. From the high performer's perspective, they eventually feel over-worked, underpaid, and unappreciated, which may lead to other issues. So managers and supervisors, though it's easier for you to constantly give additional tasks and projects to your most trusted employee, you are expected to train and develop ALL employees in your charge. Delegate work in a manner that maximizes the productivity and talents of ALL your direct reports. Not just the ones who are easier to deal with.

Now, back to what I was saying... unchallenging work.

I once had a job with a very well-known university. November 2003, I began in the medical records department as a temporary employee and was hired on full-time. I'm a hard worker and a fast learner, and within one year, I became one of the department trainers and was one of the floaters who cross-trained in other positions so I could provide coverage as needed. If no one were out, I was not responsible for completing any work that day. I absolutely loved that job and it still holds the trophy for the best job I ever had. I worked Sunday-Thursday, was off EVERY Friday and Saturday, and Sundays were so chill, that I didn't feel like I was at work. I loved my job, my coworkers, and my supervisor. The only problem was the pay. As I stated before, I am a single mother and have been since I was 18 years old. Though I loved everything about my job, I only made $9 per hour with two growing boys at home. So, by October 2004, I moved to another department within the university to a higher paying position.

In the interview, I thought I was going to be just as challenged as I was in my previous position. I was oh so very wrong. When I started, there was another person who started the same day in the same position. I was told that we would work closely and provide backup for each other. The training plan was for one person to be trained on one task, while the other person trains on a different task. Once each person was proficient, we would switch and complete this cycle for each task in our job description.

As I stated before, I'm a fast learner. So what seemed like an efficient way to train two people, didn't work so well for me. From October 2004 to April 2005 (that's six months), I learned ONE task. I worked from 8A.M.-5P.M.; by my second week I could be done with a full day's work by 9:00A.M. 10:00 A.M. if I slowed down. I was so bored.

At first, I was like, cool. I can enroll in school, get my homework done at work, and write my business plan at work, so when I get home, I can focus on the boys. That plan only lasted a few weeks because my financial aid fell through and I didn't have money to pay tuition out of my pocket, and family was not helpful in that area, so I couldn't go to school, and I lost my motivation with my business. I had a 40 hour per week job that took five hours per week (ten hours if I were slacking) for me to complete.

I went to my supervisor and asked if she would train me on another task; I was told no because she was waiting for the other employee to master the first task she was being trained on. As you may have figured out, that never happened. Yes, six months and she didn't get the first task right and was eventually terminated. Back then, 23-year-old me didn't understand what took so long with firing an underperformer. But now I know... documentation is a beast and worse in highly bureaucratic organizations. You have to dot those "I's" and cross those "T's" to make sure you don't end up on the wrong side of a wrongful termination lawsuit. Meanwhile, I was still stuck with one task.

The office was extremely quiet, and my cubicle was tucked away in the back. I dosed off... a lot. That's when I started drinking coffee. If I weren't on the internet researching random unnecessary information all day long. I was emailing my friends back and forth. I couldn't offer help to my coworkers because I had not been trained on anything else and was apparently not allowed to learn anything else.

So I had a whole lot of idle time on my hands. To entertain myself, one day I said, "if I get drunk at work, I wonder if anyone would notice?." So I mixed coffee with Kahlua and put it in a Starbucks Frappuccino bottle and rum and coke in a 20oz coke bottle and drank it my desk.

Disclaimer: DO NOT DO DRINK ALCOHOLIC BEVERAGES AT WORK. IT IS GROUNDS FOR IMMEDIATE TERMINATION.

NOBODY noticed. I started drinking the "Starbucks" when I got to work and did my work for the day. No errors at all. By 10:00 A.M., I was a lotta bit tipsy and was sober by noon or so. Why am I putting this in a book? So y'all understand the severity of my boredom. What are they going to do? Fire me. HA!

Though I had a lot of fun entertaining myself that day, I didn't do it again and was rather disappointed that I left my previous department. So I updated the resume and proceeded to search for another job. Looking for another job became my job. By the time the other employee was terminated, I was submitting my resignation. Then after I gave my two weeks' notice, my supervisor proceeded with training me on other tasks. I mean she went all in and was training me on almost everything. But at that point, it was too late. Part of me thinks she was trying to get me to change my mind. But a bigger part of me thinks she was trying to generate a paper trail that showed I had been fully trained so she could cover herself. Either way… I didn't care because I didn't like how I was being handled from day one. Had I been treated like an individual and not held back for reasons beyond my control, things may have been different.

MANAGERS AND SUPERVISORS –

When you manage people, yes, you should have a standardized training plan but don't hold one employee back if another person is not meeting expectations. The moment my supervisor realized that her original training plan was not working, she should have adapted to the situation and allowed me to proceed with learning other aspects of the role. Had my talents been properly utilized, I probably wouldn't have left so quickly. My intrinsic motivation was not being fed and resulted in my boredom and underutilization.

When hiring employees, you should be clear with them in the interview on role expectations as well as the training plan. If a candidate is used to multi-tasking and the job you have available is much slower paced, you need to make that clear. In the interview, ask the candidate questions that require them to explain what type of work environment they thrive in and what they are looking for. Use your knowledge of the role (assuming you know) to compare the candidate's response to the actual job requirements and work environment. If they aren't a good fit, fine. Move on to the next person. Don't hire a strong candidate then end up losing them because they were not challenged, and you didn't allow them the opportunity to grow. This is misuse of company resources and an avoidable factor that contributes to high turnover costs. If you don't help them grow, you will watch them go. In the event the organization's leaders ever asked why I resigned after six months of employment, what do you think their reaction to my supervisor would have been if they found out the truth? Not a very pleasant one. Just in case you are wondering, no, I did not have an exit interview. If the people at the top knew what really goes on within their organizations, the workplace might be much different.

CHAPTER 5

OVERWORKED AND UNDERPAID

Let's go back to a statement I made earlier in the book: "Jamaevra - In lieu of your hard work, you will be receiving a merit increase of 2.5%." In Chapter 1, I discussed the first part of this statement. Now, I will focus on the second part.

It's important to understand that at the time of this statement, I was well into my third year of working for this organization, and was in the same position which I started in August of 2010. The initial pay rate for the job was $14.00 per hour. It definitely wasn't a lot of money, but was more than what I made in my previous job, which paid $11.00 per hour and was the highest paying job I had up until that point. Over time, my position naturally evolved, and I took on more responsibilities. I had not yet gone back to school to complete my bachelor's degree. After a year or so, my department expanded and there were many other positions available. I expressed my interest in moving into another role and got the run around and withdrew. Before I move on, let me explain why. Because I'm not kissing anybody's ass for any reason. I have a personal code of conduct that I hold myself to.

About nine to twelve months later, the department expanded again. This time, additional people were added to the team I was on, and three more positions were added with my job title. When these other three individuals were hired, guess who trained them and answered all of their questions. I was happy to help because I was tired of my job and someone else needed to know how to do it. At this point, I was planning my exit. The only reason I had not started the job search was because of my son, which I will discuss in greater detail later. I went to my supervisor and expressed my interest in moving to a new role because I was getting bored with my current one. At this point, this was the fourth supervisor that I had mentioned this to. I was in the same position, but my supervisors kept changing. That should tell you bad it was. Well, shortly after that conversation, she left, and I was on supervisor number five.

With supervisor number five, which happens to be the same person I discussed in Chapter 1, I again expressed my interest in learning a new role. I also expressed the need of other team members being able to fully perform my role in my absence. Now, she did attempt to have me cross train another team member, but it never quite worked out. Out of respect for that person's privacy, I won't go into more detail. So, I didn't have anyone who could back me up and my workload continued to increase.

Turns out, after I trained the other three who were added to my position, I ended up being the lowest paid one in the group by a long shot. Raises weren't enough to care about. By the time I left in October 2013, I made an astounding $15.07 per hour. Which brings me to my point.

"Jamaevra - In lieu of your hard work, you will be receiving a merit increase of 2.5%."

I had received a 2.5% raise every year, but my workload was increased by way more than 2.5%. When I received this communication, my reaction was like "So what." By the time I left that position, this is what my responsibilities included.

- Delegate and monitor department workflow; assign caseloads to approximately 100 case managers based on patient need, specialty, and capacity. Distributing more than 500 cases per day. Provide working supervision, guidance, and training to administrative staff.

- Build and maintain database complete with mental health and caregiver resources is easily accessed by mental health professionals to provide patients.
- Measure and analyze department weekly performance relating to monthly and quarterly productivity goals.
- Calculate attendance data and turnover rates, including comparisons of on-site and remote staff.
- Maintain employee records including verify professional licenses and certifications and send 90/60/30-day renewal reminders to help mental health staff remain compliant for business continuity.

When I started that position, I assigned approximately 60 cases to about 30 case managers per day. It was rare for me to receive more than 80 cases per day. Towards the end, it was over 500 cases daily distributed among about 100 case managers, many of whom were remote and in different time zones. That was just one of my responsibilities. A 2.5% raise did not begin to compensate me for my efforts. And I was STILL the lowest paid one with no one to share the workload with. So as soon as my personal life reached a certain point and I found another position, guess what I did. Resigned.

This was another example of an employer telling the employee, "You are good enough for the work but I'm not going to compensate you for efforts," without actually saying the words. If you don't pay me what I'm worth, I will find someone else who will. So after leaving that position, I completed my bachelor's degree and continued seeking promotional roles. By 2018, I made over $60,000 per year before completing my master's degree. That's a long way from $15.07 per hour (which equals $31,345 per year) in 2013. If you didn't know it, hard work does pay off. But you have to know your worth and settle for nothing less.

In recent years, there has been a lot of talk about pay inequities based on race and gender. I'm a black woman, so that's a double hit for me. This topic in the media and in the HR world truly irritates me, because people act like it's such a huge surprise KNOWING what they have been doing for decades, and HR departments allow it by incorporating this magical phrase in job descriptions, "other duties as assigned." I could probably write an entire book on that phrase and how it's used to manipulate employees.

Managers and supervisors – You should strive to keep good employees around. In terms of costs, which is the better option?

> **OPTION #1** – Fairly compensate employees for the work they actually perform and provide rewards that are meaningful, support their career growth, and reduce turnover costs.

OR

> **OPTION #2** – Deny opportunities for advancement, keep their pay low, and continue to increase their workload while increasing turnover costs.

Option #1 seems a lot better to me. Here's what most managers don't understand.

Employees are hired to advance the mission of the organization, not your mission. Many supervisors and managers treat their employees as if the employee needs you, when in fact, you need the employee. When experienced and high-performing employees leave an organization, they take their knowledge, skills, and abilities (KSAs) with them. The turnover costs associated with replacing that individual increases with length of employment.

Managers should be building teams who can further the work of the organization for years to come. If you want employees to be com-placent in what they do and their pay rate, then you should stop asking them to take on more responsibilities. If an organization is growing, it needs employees who are willing to grow with it. True leaders iden-tify and train successors so they can move on to bigger and better things. If you aren't, you are merely holding a job title and hurting your organization's ability to achieve its long-term goals.

CHAPTER 6

MICROMANAGEMENT

Before I discuss micromanagement, let me first define MANAGE-MENT. My definition of MANAGEMENT is the coordination of all available company resources (financial, natural, technological, human, etc.) to accomplish business objectives that have been outlined in support of the strategic goals of the organization. There are many different styles of management. Each manager will have their own management style because each manager is different. The level of skill, tact, and quality of management will also vary and is dependent upon the individual manager.

Now let's define MICROMANAGEMENT. My definition of MICROMANAGEMENT is the act of maintaining control by applying excessive attention to minor details. Here's an example.

You are a manager in a call center and your team needs to be available to accept phone calls at all times during business hours. As team members are human, they will need to use the restroom at some point. Because this is a call center, team members are required to log off their phones using a reason code designated for restroom breaks and takes them out of the call queue. You notice that one employee was logged out of her phone using the restroom reason code for a duration of 7 minutes and 14 seconds. Upon her return, you email the employee and ask why they were in the restroom for so long. That, my dear, is micromanagement. Micromanagement comes into play when you start focusing on things that do not matter.

There is a fine line between management and micromanagement. As a supervisor, I have had a couple of instances where I have had to micromanage some of my direct reports. For the record, I hated it. These employees were regularly falling behind in their work and missing deadlines. These same employees would request overtime or work through their lunch to get caught up on their work on a regular basis. Even though I do it, I do not like my employees working through their breaks or lunches and I do not want them to work overtime regularly. As the leader, I feel I should pitch in when extra help is needed and work the longer hours. Here is my viewpoint on overtime. Overtime pay should only be utilized during periods of increased work requirements or when there is a temporary staff shortage and shouldn't be an ongoing occurrence. When I have an employee who is regularly working more than 40 hours per week, I need to evaluate their workload and ensure that they are effectively managing their time and resources. Here's the scenario.

At the time, I supervised a team of 11 individuals. We were fully staffed. Nine of my employees were busy throughout the day, but not working overtime and not missing deadlines. Two people were regularly falling behind in their work. That means that 18% of my team's productivity was not being completed on time. Not cool. Now one person would reach out to her coworkers for assistance while the other one would just let things fall through the cracks and apologize afterwards. My supervisor wanted to reassign their workloads to other people. As I have stated before, I am against this practice and felt that since I was the supervisor, I needed to do my job and develop my employees who were struggling. If I didn't, that meant I was failing as a leader. So I met with each employee individually, to let them know what I had been noticing and tried to figure out what was going on that was interfering with their productivity. Both revealed they were having issues with time management and acknowledged that they need to make improvements. The first step, "Acceptance," was taken care of.

From there, I gave them suggestions on how to manage their time. I also required that they keep a task list and send that to me weekly. This could have been called micromanaging, but this was actually managing. The reason it's not micromanaging is because the employees had displayed an inability to manage their workloads without my involvement. The task list was for me to actually monitor their actual productivity, documentation supporting their performance improvement plans, and to identify areas of improvement as necessary. Within a few weeks, both employees improved in the area of time management and improved performance. At this point, I no longer required the task list and resumed business as usual.

When it comes to micromanagement, it's exhausting and a waste of my time. If you work for me, I will trust you to do the job you are paid to do until the moment that you prove that you can no longer be trusted. If I cannot trust you to do your job and have to constantly check in on you, then you should no longer work for me. Period.

In the case of the task list for my direct reports, if they had continued to poorly manage their time then it would be safe to assume that the job was not a good fit for them, and I would need to take appropriate steps to discontinue the work relationship and identify suitable replacements. Had I required all my employees to send me task lists regardless of their performance and productivity, then I would have been micromanaging my team.

Speaking from personal experience, micromanaging is belittling. Especially to high performers. When you have a natural internal drive to do good job, being micromanaged is demeaning. It also proves to your employees that you do not trust them. As a leader, I know you have other responsibilities to take care of. You would have more time to manage the business if you didn't focus so much on what you are paying other people to do. The more you show your employees that you trust them, the more productive they will be. Micromanagers create more unnecessary work for themselves and drive good employees away.

CHAPTER 7

TOXIC WORK ENVIRONMENT

At work, as in your personal life, you teach people how to treat you. People can only treat you as good or bad as you allow yourself to be treated. I am a firm believer that I will NEVER need a job badly enough to allow myself to be disrespected or mistreated in any way. Unfortunately, many people don't share the same belief and put up with abusive behaviors at work that they would not ordinarily tolerate out of fear of losing their job. This is human and no one can blame you for doing what you have to do to provide for yourself and your family. But many people do not know that they have the right to go to work and be treated with dignity and respect. After observing managers and supervisors in my past workplaces, I have realized that many individuals in position of authority behave the way they do for three reasons.

1. They don't know any better.
2. They believe that there are no consequences for their actions and the rules don't apply to them.
3. They are on a power trip.

Contrary to popular workplace practices, when you step into a role where you are responsible for others, everything you do and say can potentially increase legal risk to the organization you work for, and ignorance of the law is not an acceptable defense. If you don't believe me, research it. As a leader, you should ensure your actions are a positive contribution to your organization and not increasing the level of toxicity in your workplace.

There are many elements that contribute to a toxic work environment. Bullying, sexual harassment, racism, sexism, ageism, gossiping, retaliation, ostracizing, and just plain unprofessionalism are just a few issues that are common in toxic workplaces. For the purposes of this book, I'm going to focus on the one element that irritates me the most, bullying. As I am a black woman, you may have thought I was going to go with racism or sexism. But no, BULLYING in the workplace is the one element that tap dances on my last nerve because it is rooted in deception and shows how devious a person can be. Racism and sexism, while still disgusting, can be simply explained with biases and one's misguided perception that they are superior to another person because of characteristics that neither person has control over.

My definition of workplace bullying is when a person in position of authority uses the power and influence of their position to intimidate an employee with less authority. Victims of bullying are not limited to lower-level employees, but it is more apparent because lower level employees are more likely to turnover than executives. Line staff can be bullied by supervisors, supervisors can be bullied by managers, managers can be bullied by directors, directors can be bullied by vice presidents, vice presidents can be bullied by presidents, and presidents can be bullied by CEOs, CTOs, COOs, CFOs, and every other chief executive position. While bullying can occur at all levels of an organization, the degree of complexity increases as the level of authority increases. Despite this, bullying at all levels comes down to one thing: intimidate or scare the other person into doing what you want them to do. But in order to scare someone, first you have to be sure they have the ability to do what you want, and next you need to know what they fear most. To bully any employee, a manager, supervisor, or other person in authority will figure out who their most talented/high-performing employees are and work to figure out something to use against them. Low and under-performing employees don't have to worry too much about being bullied because they have nothing to give in return. It's simple psychology. So if you are a strong employee, be cautious when someone in position of authority starts asking you personal questions or taking you to lunch. In some cases, these can be harmless conversations and gestures, and your supervisor may just want to build rapport and trust. The way you will notice their true intentions is by how the conversation starts. If they go straight for it and say, "tell me something about yourself outside of work," then you may want to put that guard up. If at any point, they start talking negatively about another colleague, you can be sure they will do the same to you. There is a huge difference in the actions of a manager/supervisor who simply wants to get to know you and one who has ill will towards you.

As a leader, I try to be someone who my employees can trust and want to get to know them. But I leave it on their terms. I hold one-on-one meetings that are intended to be private coaching sessions to help improve their performance and career development. But over time, I have also had the pleasure of getting to know each and every one of them. Some employees tell me personal information upfront, while others take longer to open up. Either way is fine with me, because I let my employees take the wheel in this area and I support them as needed.

Now for the supervisor who has ill intentions.

From 2010-2013, I worked for a health insurance provider. This is the same position that I mentioned earlier where my supervisor changed five times but I did not change jobs. When I interviewed for the position, I interviewed with a man who was easy to get along with and I liked a lot, but after my first week, I was reassigned to supervisor number two. But wasn't officially told until I asked for assistance from supervisor number one and was redirected. Now, I can tell you, if I had interviewed with supervisor number two, I'm quite certain I would not have been offered the position in the first place. I got a VERY off-putting vibe from her. She could be extremely nice, but have you ever met someone who was so nice that it seemed fake? Yeah, that was her. As I said earlier, I am a single parent and have been for a long time. If you have ever been in a conversation with me for longer than ten minutes, I will more than likely mention my kids whom I adore, and I have never been a single parent that felt ashamed. That's the hand life dealt me, and the Most High God apparently trusted me enough to manage it, and I am damn proud of it. Anyway… I don't believe I told my supervisor directly that I had kids. I think she overheard a conversation with my coworker and asked me if I had children and if I were married, and I responded. In my first one-on-one meeting with supervisor #2, her first question to me was "Do you ever talk to your baby daddy?" Damn, just straight out with it. The fact that this was a white woman (the supervisor) asking a black woman (the employee) this question at work during work time comes with its own set of problems, and I could have had her fired and gotten a FAT check if I wanted to. But like so many employees do (especially black ones), I didn't report it. But I did respond, "What does that have to do with work?" and she responded, "Oh, I just want to use this time to get to know you better." I then said, "Well, that's an inappropriate question, but if you must know, no, I don't talk to him. We were supposed to get married but didn't." She said, "Oh I'm sorry." I said "Why are you sorry? I'm not. He was abusive and leaving him was the best decision I ever made. Do you want to know anything else?" She then changed the subject. Remember what I said earlier about supervisors not knowing what they should or shouldn't do. This is a prime example. If I had reported this, her not knowing would not have been acceptable. As I was still within my first month of employment, the one-on-one meeting should have been aimed at making sure I was understanding the demands of the role, not trying to figure out the circumstances of the relationship with the person who impregnated me. So that guard of mine went up and never came down. This is an example of a situation of a supervisor with malicious intent.

Outside of that unpleasant one-on-one meeting, I never really had any other problems with supervisor number two. But the information she received was used against me by supervisors numbers three through five. Anytime I spoke up or did not act like a puppet, I would get the "Well, you don't want to lose your job" comment, but reached my breaking point with the manager of supervisor number four.

When I started reporting to supervisor number four, she and her manager were constantly harassing me. Every week I was being pulled away from my desk over some bullshit. First it was, I wasn't doing my job fast enough and I needed to be done with a particular task by 10:00 A.M., even though I started work at 8:00 A.M. and the workload had more than doubled. The task under scrutiny was assigning new cases to mental health providers. I was told I that had one minute to assign each new case. I said "fine" and left that meeting. The next week I had another meeting, where I was told, "Someone said you said something offensive, but I can't tell you who it was, who you were talking to, or what you said." I said, "So how am I supposed to resolve the issue?" I was told to be mindful of what I said. Okay. So I stopped talking to everybody. Not even a good morning. I talked to one person on my team (who I am still friends with); if you weren't her, you got nothing out of me. Everyone else was limited to email conversation. I sent an email to my supervisor requesting that anyone who needed to talk to me talk to her first without approaching me directly. They hated it. But if I were so offensive, then it shouldn't have been a problem. I redirected everybody to my supervisor and her manager and stopped being so helpful. Honestly, it was so much easier for me.

TIP: If you ever find yourself in a similar situation, you have every right to limit contact as reasonably required to perform your duties. Technically, other managers and colleagues are supposed to consult with your direct supervisor before requesting anything work-related. In my situation, I didn't need to talk to complete my duties.

Now if you know me, you know ignoring people has never been an issue for me. I came through the door in the morning with headphones on and kept them on until I left. After all, I had two young men to take care of and a financial goal to meet. The way I saw it, if you are aiming to terminate my employment, fine, but it won't be because you caught me slipping.

TIP: If you ever feel your supervisor is aiming to terminate you but they don't have a valid reason, just know the two easiest reasons to terminate anyone are Attendance and Insubordination. These are also two reasons that will cause your unemployment claim to be denied. Most unemployment insurance claims are valid as long as you lost your job through no fault of your own. So when they start messing with you, no matter how mad you are, do not let them see it and do not start calling in. Come to work on time, return from breaks/lunches on time, and leave on time. Make them find a valid reason to terminate you on their own. Don't give them the ammunition or the gun and make it easier for them to pull the trigger.

Back to the story...

After these incidents, I got pulled into meetings a few more times, but the last one took the cake, and I was fed up. Keep in mind, I still hadn't been reporting to supervisor number four for a full two months.

The situation started on a Friday morning. I remember it clearly because it was the Friday before my birthday, which was the following Tuesday. Here's something about me: I don't allow my birthday to be celebrated at work, but I also don't come to work. Before supervisor number four had moved into her role, I was scheduled to be off the day before, the day of, and the day after my birthday. Friday morning, I got an email from my supervisor's manager requesting that I develop a report that compared unplanned absences of in-house and remote staff. The deadline to complete it was the upcoming Monday after-noon. The last line in the email said, "Please let me know what you need from me to make this happen."

Well at the time, I didn't know who all the remote employees were and would need to do some research. So my response said:

"Hi. I would be happy to provide this data but don't have every-thing I need to get this completed in the requested timeframe. I don't know off-hand nor do I have access to a list of all the individuals who are classified as remote employees and would need to do some pre-liminary research to figure this out. But if you already have this in-formation and can send it by noon today, I could possibly complete the report by the close of business today. If not, then the deadline of Monday is not feasible as I won't be able to provide this information until Thursday because I am out of the office Monday-Wednesday."

I got pulled into yet another meeting. My supervisor's manager basically said I was being insubordinate and expecting them to do the work for me. I said, "Your email said to let you know what I needed to make this happen and I told you. If you didn't want to provide as-sistance or don't know how, you shouldn't have offered. On top of that, it is not my fault you don't know when your team members are scheduled to be out. How was I supposed to know that the previous manager didn't relay that information? As a manager and the new-comer, you should have taken it upon yourself to ask if anyone had any upcoming time off so you can plan work accordingly." She then said okay and told me that a completion date of Thursday was fine. I thought it was over; it was not.

A week after I returned to work and completed the report, I got pulled into another meeting. This time, she was on a whole new level. This (for lack of a better word) bitch went back to the refusing work accusation. She started by thanking me for completing the report but stated she was disappointed in my approach, and I initially refused to complete the task as requested.

She had an agenda and everything. I guess I could have considered that meeting as my "verbal warning." I lost it, and I let her and my direct supervisor have it. Everything I had bottled up since I started reporting to them came out. In short, I basically said, "This is where this ends. I come here and do my job and I don't say a word to anybody and that's not good enough. You say I'm insubordinate, but I still completed the request and every other request. On top of that, I have tried to help you because I know you are new, and I know the background information on a lot. From now on, I'm done. When I see you to struggling on an issue, I'll keep quiet and watch you fall on your face. Since I'm so offensive when I talk, don't expect my help. It is not my fault that you two do not know what is going on and I should not have to spell out everything to my supervisor like I'm talking to a two-year-old. You want me to respect you as my supervisor then earn it. But what I will not do is continue to be pulled into meetings and disrespected. You don't have to truly respect me, but you better let me think you do. If I am so bad at what I do and so hard to get along with, you are welcome to terminate me. But you won't because you know I'm the best thing on this team and you can't. If you don't have anything to validate these accusations, this meeting is over." They looked at each other. I got up, walked out, and went to my desk and put my documentation together. I was waiting because I knew a write-up was coming. After how I talked to them, I deserved it, but the saga escalated even more.

A couple days later, I was scheduled for a meeting with my supervisor, her manager, and HR. This was finally an official meeting. But my supervisor's manager wasn't done. She was still determined to write me up for insubordination. So she took the email conversation that I mentioned earlier and cut bits and pieces of my response into a separate Word document. She added a cute little border around it and everything. The copy of her initial email request read exactly like the original conversation, but when you got to my response, it seemed like I told her I was not going to complete the requested task. Everything else about time off, not having access to source information, or even me saying if she already had the information I could complete the report prior to the requested deadline was deleted. So, I just let this chick talk and talk and talk. The HR rep was on the phone because the HR office was in another state. Now, the whole time the manager was talking, my direct supervisor didn't say a word. The HR rep asked if I wanted to speak on my behalf and I said yes. First, I apologized for the way I spoke to them in the prior meeting, but stated that I felt that I was provoked and this document is a prime example of what I'm talking about and what drove me to react the way I did. I stated that the document was a forgery and did not detail the entire email conversation. I asked the manager if she really thought I had forgotten my email response. She said, "The other emails don't matter, the only thing that matters is what this says." I said, "No, if you're going to say something, tell everything. Before we move forward, I want to add my own documentation and comments." The manager started to say no, but HR chimed in and said, "Yes, you can. Can you have it to me within the next two hours?" I responded, "Yes." HR said, "Okay, send me your comments and documentation, and I will reach out to continue once I have reviewed." I went to my desk and gathered all of the documentation I had, my comments, the original email conversation of that cut and paste job by the manager, and a copy of the report that was completed. I sent copies of awards I received for high performance, performance evaluations, emails expressing gratitude, and compliments I had received from other managers, coworkers, and the director of the department. Because I already had it all together, it probably took 20-30 minutes to add the final piece and send. After I sent everything I had, HR called my manager and direct supervisor. I'm assuming he wasn't too happy about that fraudulent email document she tried to use, because when I was called into the conference room, I was told we were disregarding it. HR explained that after reviewing the documentation and comments I sent, he was not moving forward with the claim that I was insubordinate. But they still had the issue of my behavior in the prior meeting. He laid out the terms of my disciplinary action, which was six months, and asked if we all agreed. We agreed, signed, and that was that. Honestly, I didn't have another issue with supervisor number four.

This is an example of bullying that could have gone a different direction if:

1. I didn't have the appropriate documentation to support my counter claim that I was being provoked.
2. I had started having bad attendance.
3. I discussed my situation with co-workers. Yes, venting to co-workers can cause issues because it can be said that you are contributing to a hostile work environment. I know it's hard, but sometimes silence is your best friend.
4. I did not know my rights.

My documentation not only proved that the manager created a fraudulent document, but also supported my claim that I was being provoked and that the repeated meetings and unjustified accusations were creating a hostile work environment. Add in the fact that the manager was white and I'm black, and you have the start to a EEOC investigation that probably would have ended in my favor. One of the main purposes of the Human Resources Department is to protect the organization, not the managers within it. It was made apparent that the manager involved in my issue was creating a hostile environment and I had enough documentation to prove it. While I was wrong for verbally abusing my supervisor and her manager, I still would have had a valid legal claim if it had gotten to that point. Documentation is key. Always Cover Your Ass.

A couple of months later, supervisor number four resigned without having another position. Prior to her leaving, we had gotten to know each other a lot better, and I realized she was not the evil person I thought she was. Her manager was the puppet master, and she was also being bullied. Just in case you are wondering, yes, I completed my disciplinary action. In fact, after a few weeks into it, supervisor number stopped meeting with me about it because she said it was a "misunderstanding" and was unfair. When I left in 2013, it was a voluntary resignation.

Then came supervisor number five that was mentioned earlier. She was a bully, but she was much more subtle. These are the ones that you really have to watch, because they seem very nice but will stab you in the back as soon as you let your guard down. They are opportunists.

Earlier, I mentioned that the number of cases that I needed to assign daily started at approximately 60 and increased to over 500, and there was no change to my other duties. One day, supervisor number five sent me an email and said she and the manager would need to meet with me. Apparently, I had not been completing assigning the 500 cases fast enough. They pulled out some old reference material. Remember the meeting I had with supervisor number four and her manager where I was told I needed to complete assignments by 10:00am? Well, that was brought up in the meeting, and I was told that I was not meeting expectations and my performance would need to improve. I asked what was wrong with my performance and they said that I was taking too long to get assignments out each day. I was completing this one task much later than 10:00 A.M. and was actually getting this task completed 1:30 P.M. daily.

After my supervisor and manager finished telling me what the problem was, I defended myself. I said that the 10:00 A.M. deadline that I was given was set when the average number of cases to be assigned was 60 per day, and it was not possible to assign 500 cases in the same amount of time. The manager, of course, proceeded with trying to make it seem like I was refusing work and said I should think about my kids before I did so. See how they were so eager to use their knowledge about me being a single parent against me? At this point, I had learned to refrain from verbal debates and put everything in writing, so I held my tongue. I calmly said, "Let me do some research and figure out what to do." I asked if they had anything else to discuss, they said no, we left the conference room, and I returned to my desk to begin my research.

I went through my emails and found the email where I was given the 10:00 A.M. daily deadline and reviewed it word for word. The email also stated that it should take one minute to assign each case. This is what I used to defend myself and I composed and sent an email that recapped the meeting but also contained my counter argument. I don't remember the email word for word, but I know it went a little something like this:

Hi Supervisor Number Five and Manager,

Thank you for meeting with me to discuss your concerns about my performance. In this meeting you informed me that my work performance has not been satisfactory as I have been completing daily assignments by 1:30 P.M. and not 10:00 A.M. as previously instructed.

After reviewing the email where the 10:00am deadline was set, I came across other information that should be considered in relation to this task. The email (attached) also states that it should take one minute to assign each case. With an average of 500 cases that need to be assigned daily, this means that it should take 8.33 hours (500 cases/60 minutes) to complete this one task. I am currently completing this task by 1:30 P.M. By the standards that have been previously set, I am completing this task more than three hours ahead of schedule, in addition to completing my other tasks which I assume are satisfactory as you have not brought any additional concerns to my attention.

At this point, I do not see how I can go any faster without sacrificing quality and reducing accuracy. If you would like to demonstrate how this task can be completed sooner, I would be happy to observe your process.

Please let me know if there are any details that I missed.

Thanks, Jamaevra

End of email. When I received the response, all I was told was to continue what I had been doing. They may not have liked what I said, but they couldn't do much about it. I was already doing more than what I was supposed to be doing in an eight-hour workday, and they could not require more at that point. If they had attempted to write me up on the basis of not meeting performance expectations, there would have been no justification and HR would not have supported it. I also asked for a demonstration on how to complete the task faster and they did not follow through with the request. Not doing so meant that supervisor number five did not meet the HR requirement of taking the necessary steps to improve performance. When a supervisor tries to terminate an employee for not meeting performance expectations, they must show that they took reasonable steps to help the employee succeed. An employee requesting additional guidance qualifies as reasonable steps to improve performance.

As a supervisor, employee development is your responsibility. If employees are not meeting performance expectations, you have to prove it. It is not good enough to just tell employees what to do; you should also be able to tell or show them how to do it. If you can't, you should at least direct them on where to receive the guidance they need. This reduces the risk of a wrongful termination lawsuit to the organization.

If you are being bullied at work, you need to learn how to stand up for yourself. Verbal confrontations are not going to help your situation. When they made the comment about my kids, I could have lost it. But I would have been at fault. Holding your human side back is difficult but necessary. Once you understand that you are only being bullied because you are good at your job and the bully merely wants to scare you into doing more than you should be to make them look better, the battle gets a little easier.

When you are confronting your bully at work, be sure to follow these guidelines. Be sure to adjust to your individual situation as needed.

Familiarize yourself with your employers' Human Resources policies and procedure. These are typically included in the employee handbook. If the situation does not improve, you will need to follow the conflict-resolution procedures as outlined. In most cases, the law requires employees to prove that they followed company HR policies and procedures and the organization has not taken the appropriate steps to resolve the issue. Making sure you are aware of the company's policies and procedures will help you take the appropriate steps to protect yourself and resolve your issue. Knowledge is power.

Refrain from verbal confrontations as much as possible. When you are upset, you may say some things that could get you in trouble later.

Recap all meetings in an email. Bullies love to have meetings and talk, because in the event of a complaint, verbal conversations are hard to prove. You do not have to wait for your supervisor to document conversations.

When you recap the meeting, summarize the meeting from start to finish. If you are stating a problem, support it with other documentation and attach it to the email.

At the end of the email, include a line that requires your supervisor/manager to verify that you accurately summarized the meeting. Something like what I said in my email, "Please let me know if there are any details that I missed" should work. Be sure to be accurate and do not add anything that was not discussed. To make it easier, record meetings and use the recording to make sure you have included everything or simply take notes. Whatever works best for you. If you choose to record meetings, research relevant laws in your state before doing so. The law can help you determine if you should only use the recording for the sake of accurately transcribing meetings or if you can save for possible use in arbitration or court.

Be professional but also assertive. Remove emotion and keep it focused on the business need. When I stated that, "I do not see how

I can go any faster without sacrificing quality and reducing accuracy," this was supporting the business need. If my supervisor had told me to work faster and errors were increased as a result, the burden would have been on them to explain to HR if they attempted to terminate me or if upper management had an issue.

Always end the email with "thank you." While you may not want to thank them, make sure you cannot be accused of being unprofessional or rude. The goal is to prove that they are out of line, not get out of line yourself.

You may feel that if you just keep your head down and do your job, the problem will go away. But it won't. Not dealing with a problem will only make it worse. The only way to defeat a bully is to stand up to them.

CHAPTER 8

LIFE

Many times, life can be the driving force that keeps you in a job that you hate longer than you would like. Life can also cause you to leave a job that you absolutely love sooner than expected. I once had a manager (one of the few that I actually liked) who said, "We work to live, not live to work." This statement is very true, but you wouldn't know it by observing how poorly many employees are treated in the workplace. More often than not, employees are treated as if the employer is doing them a favor by allowing them to work there. In reality, the employee is doing the employer a favor by coming to work. Especially if the employee is a high performer. If you don't believe me, name one company that would be in business if no one worked there. Can you think of one? Didn't think so.

As an employee (good or bad), you are free to choose to go to work and earn your paycheck, or you can choose to not work and increase your financial and life struggles. Either way, everyone makes a choice when they go to work. As a leader, I believe it is my duty to create an environment where my employees don't dread being. Unfortunately, a lot of supervisors, whether intentional or not, actively contribute to work environments that employees despise. Thus increasing absenteeism, workplace toxicity, and turnover.

Earlier, I mentioned a position where I was told "Jamaevra - In lieu of your hard work, you will be receiving a merit increase of 2.5%." The 2.5% increase was a joke and a slap in the face, but I accepted it because of my life circumstances at the time. As I have said, I have been a single parent since I was 18 and I have two other people who rely on me and will be unwillingly affected by the consequences of my actions. While a bigger paycheck would have been lovely, money was not the driving factor for me remaining in that position at that point in time. Here was my life situation. Two kids, one that I decided to homeschool and the other who was in the fifth grade. The biggest concern was my fifth grader (the youngest). The school he attended was less than two miles away from where we lived, had no bus transportation, and was in a really good school district. The job I had, while the pay was low, I worked from home three days a week, and the physical office was maybe one mile away from where I lived. When I was in the office or working from home, I could take a late lunch, pick my baby up from school, and take him home without a problem. Working from home also allowed me to make sure my oldest who was home schooling was actually do his work and not playing video games. In the event my car broke down, I was within walking distance to work, my son's school, and the grocery store. That apartment was strategically chosen for those reasons. When I make decisions, I evaluate "what if" scenarios and think about long-term repercussions. I'm not impulsive at all.

As far as the job, I couldn't stand working there. As in most cases, it wasn't the job that I hated; it was almost everything else. They pay was low and the culture was not ideal, but it was convenient. By the time I received this 2.5% increase, it was my third year working there and my youngest was in the fifth grade. So the plan was to stay with that employer until he went to middle school and bus transportation was available. That's exactly what I did. So in May of his fifth grade year, I began my job search. By August, I found a higher paying job that also allowed me to gain more experience, but the next employer's

HR department was so slow that I didn't leave until October.

Before developing my exit strategy, I tried to advance. The first time was about a year into my employment and our department had been approved to expand. Additional positions were created, and I had initially expressed interest in one of the newly created positions. I was given the run around and withdrew my application. A few months later, I expressed interest to my supervisor about wanting to learn more of the data analytics and explained that I wanted to do more. She thought it was a good idea, but then she got fed up and left. I expressed the same interest to her replacement and was not given the opportunity to advance, but she did make sure I took on some analytical responsibilities. I don't think she thought that I was serious about wanting to do something completely different until I handed her my resignation.

Managers and supervisors – when an employee comes to you and asks for promotional opportunities, don't take this lightly and think you can give them additional responsibilities without officially promoting them in title and pay. When this happened, all I did was add the additional responsibilities to my resume, which made it easier for me to market myself and move on to the next employer. Not taking an employee's desire to advance seriously is much more costly to you than you think. Get over yourself and start thinking about the big picture. If you don't pay an employee for their efforts and don't recognize the need to fully promote them, you are basically training them for another employer. If they stick around, don't believe that they can't or won't leave. Like with me, there could be other forces keeping them in their current role. But as soon as those circumstances change, they may be walking out the door.

We have discussed an example of how life can keep employees in a position that they hate for longer than desired. Now let's talk about how life can cause an employee to leave a position they love.

At the age of 22, I began working as a temp in the medical records department of a well-known university medical center. After seven months of being a temp, I was hired as a full-time employee. I loved my job. I worked Sunday-Thursday. The work was challenging, the benefits were great, my supervisor was amazing, my coworkers were awesome, and the overall culture was good. But there was one problem. I made $9.00 per hour. After the annual raise, my pay went up to a whopping $9.87 per hour. But I had two kids. I didn't receive child support and was told that I made too much money to receive food stamps or housing assistance. I looked into subsidized housing, but nothing was immediately available. Waiting lists ranged from one and a half to eight years. I wasn't going to wait nor plan to be financially challenged that long. Not going to work for me. Still to this day, I have a hard time believing that there are people in this world who will wait eight years to receive low-income housing. That's just sad to me. Anywho… my parents helped me as much as they could, but I was an adult, and my kids were my responsibility. So my only option was to make more money and I left for a higher paying job.

When I started my quest to increase my paycheck, I started running into jobs and managers that I couldn't stand. Isn't that funny? Remember the song "Mo'money, mo' problems" by The Notorius B.I.G.? Ain't that the damn truth. But will that ever stop me from striving to make more money and improving myself? Not likely. Every problem that arises is just an opportunity to improve your conflict management skills.

Managers and supervisors, unfortunately there will be times where you can be doing everything right and you will still lose good employees. In my situation, the low pay rate was beyond the control of my manager. That was the compensation structure she was given. I was not the only person who left that department in search of a higher paying position. The revolving door is why many people started as temps and moved into full-time role as a way of managing turnover costs. Being the great manager she was, she recognized that her department was a "foot in the door" department, and she supported her employees who desired career growth. She helped me and many others before and after me obtain promotional opportunities within the organization.

As a manager, you should understand the nature of the positions that you oversee. If you are over a low-paying department, don't expect good employees to stick around forever. Your goal should be to train and develop talented employees to advance within the organization. Once you come to terms with the fact that part of your job is to help the organization (as a whole) retain talented employees and not just your department or division, you can develop a management strategy that supports that. Here's an example.

I worked with a manager who was hiring a front desk position in a large healthcare system. The position required someone who was friendly and self-motivated to greet visitors, answer phones, order office supplies and coffee, sort mail, restock breakroom supplies, process expense reports, pay invoices, and work on special projects as necessary. Prior to hiring this candidate, the manager structured the positions in their department in a manner that limited vertical opportunities. Candidate #1 met the educational and skills requirements of the position but was unsure about their long-term career goals within the organization, because they had never worked in healthcare and wanted to gain a better understanding of the organizational structure so she can figure out her individual career path. For the front desk, this was very reasonable. Candidate #2, who was ultimately selected, had just completed a master's degree in health administration and was currently working for a non-profit healthcare organization that had a very low pay scale, which was almost equivalent to the salary for the front desk position. The manager told me that they preferred Candidate #2 because Candidate #1 was unsure about her career, and even though Candidate #2 had a master's degree the departmental structure limited opportunities for growth, which showed me that the limited opportunities for growth was intentional. Crazy.

On their first day, I met the new hire and they asked, "how long do I need to be in a position before I qualify for promotional opportunities in other departments?" I told her that the requirement was six months. You guessed it, six months down the road, Candidate #2 was gone (promotional opportunity with another department), and the manager was once again in search of someone to fill the front desk position.

Had this manager been thinking long-term and had any type of foresight, they would have seen this coming. To me, candidate #1 would have been a much better fit. After all, it was the front desk of one department and not the hospital administrator. It is unreasonable to hire someone with a master's degree and work experience, and expect them to work at the front desk for an extended period of time. It's also naïve to believe that any employee who is seeking a promotional opportunity won't leave your department or organization.

When you are hiring for an entry-level position, hire someone with entry level skills and create a structure which allows the employee to grow as the position evolves. This way, the employee continues to develop, learns new skills, and will probably stick around for more than six months. If the candidate possesses the basic skills to do the job and has the desire to grow, that should be enough. And you won't have to interview, hire, and train new people every few months. Shocking... I know.

Having a structure that supports growth reduces the likelihood of an employee leaving a job they love because the demands of life outgrew their jobs ability to meet those demands. While some turnover is natural and healthy, you shouldn't have a constant revolving door.

CHAPTER 9

AMBITION

There is one characteristic that sets all good employees apart from underperforming employees. Ambition. According to the Oxford Dictionary, ambition is defined as "a strong desire to do or to achieve something, typically requiring determination and hard work." Not all ambitious people have a desire for higher positions; some people just have a strong desire to do a great job. Speaking for myself, my ambition keeps me up at night. I have goals that I think about day in and day out. Sometimes, I can't sleep because just thinking about the things I want to achieve in life keeps me up. The only way I fall asleep is for me to get up a write down my thoughts. There are times that I can think about my goals so much that I will get a headache. Not everyone will be able to relate to this. If you are someone who wants reward without the work, you probably do not understand. If you are someone who does not have a goal beyond "taking it one day at a time" or keeping up with what someone else is doing, you probably will not understand. But if you are constantly thinking about something and just the thought brings you joy no matter what is going on in your life, you know exactly what I mean.

A couple of years before I left a prior employer, I had a dream that scared the mess out of me. I was driving to work like any other morning but when I got to work, I put the accelerator to the floor and drove directly into the side of the parking garage. The car was completely totaled, but I got out the car and walked away without a scratch. I believe that was God's way of telling me, "You are going nowhere here, but if you trust me and get out, you will be fine." I eventually quit in early 2019 and I was miserable day in and day out until I did. My paycheck had grown significantly but still not what I felt I deserved. At the time of my resignation, my annual salary was over $63,000. Pretty good, but not good enough. I had benefits that were okay, but could have been better. My responsibilities were challenging, but I still was drastically underutilized. My ideas were not supported. Problems were never resolved, and I was never allowed to take steps towards making the necessary improvements. I was even told by my supervisor that my efforts were a waste of time.

There were times that I would get so mad in meetings with my supervisor that I would cry. Now let me explain something. The tears were not because my feelings were hurt or that I felt weak. The tears started flowing because I was frustrated from the level of restraint required to keep myself from physically hurting my manager. I have never worked with anyone whom I despised to that degree. Before I left, I had gotten to the point where I declined meeting requests from my manager. At this point, I did not care because the law was on my side. I now understand how people snap and resort to violence at work. If you know anything about HR, you know a hostile work environment is always taken seriously. Why? To reduce the threat of workplace violence, bad publicity, and lawsuits. I talked to HR, I had emails, recordings, and other documentation backing me up, and if I had stayed, I would have had a nice lawsuit. But I didn't care enough to keep it going. I needed my sanity back and stress gone ASAP. Be that as it may, I knew this was an area where I needed drastic improvement. Sometimes you encounter people in life whose sole purpose is to help you develop a particular muscle that you will need to overcome something later in life. By the time I left, I had greatly developed in that area because of some advice my oldest son gave me. He said, "Mom, if you stop expecting so much from people, you wouldn't get so mad. Just lower your expectations." My oldest son is a man of few words, but what he says makes so much sense, and that's what I did. Unfortunately, I was not okay with adopting that attitude. It was a good temporary fix, but I could not do that for the rest of my career. I have about 20 years left in the workforce and needed to start working towards my true ambitions. For me to be happy at work, I needed a role that allowed me to be who I am. I also needed a manager who was a leader. I have a good amount of work experience, but I have lot of years left in the workforce, and in order to get where I want to go, I need to work with people who I can learn from and not someone who needs their ego stroked.

Before joining this department, I worked for a different department. I was miserable there too. I reported to a manager I couldn't stand, and my talents were severely underutilized. I was overworked, underpaid, and severely stressed. So stressed that I ended up on FMLA because my heart rhythm was off. This was something I didn't take lightly. I am a fairly healthy person, was 34 years old, and had only been in the hospital to give birth and be born. This was a no-no for me. My doctor said, "Jamaevra, I only see you for your annual physical and now you come in for an urgent appointment and have too long in between heartbeats. Your body is just warning you that something worse is about to happen." She took me off work for six weeks, but advised me that I need to really think about whether or not I was going back. I still had kids to take care of, and unfortunately, I didn't find another job before the end of my six weeks. As the only adult in the house, I went back to work, but I promised myself and my kids that I will quit a job before I ever felt remotely the way I felt when I went on sick leave. About a month after returning to work, I transferred to the final department that I just told you about for a promotional position. Remember when I said the law would have been on my side? Prior medical leave due to stress in someone who had no pre-existing conditions, on top of a hostile environment was solid. But my previous health scare is also the reason why I just walked away. I'm the only parent my boys have, and I will not let something as trivial a job take me away from them. Just in case you are wondering, I made a full recovery and haven't had any issues since.

After leaving that organization, I took some time off of work, finished my master's degree, and took the time to look for an employer that allowed me to be myself and promoted a culture of learning and growth. And I found it. I absolutely love my current employer and it is everything I could have ever asked for. From promotional opportunities, to benefits, to perks, to managers who are true leaders, I couldn't ask for anything more. But I know this is also only temporary because my ultimate goal is to run my own business.

Since I was a little kid, I never desired to work for anyone else. As a matter of fact, the only reason I ever started working for someone else is because I had children young and it was a necessity. Now the children are young men who are in college and can pretty much take care of themselves, it's time for me to do me. While I am thankful I have found a good fit with a organization that will nurture my development and meets my financial needs, deep down I know it's temporary because I STILL constantly dream and think about something else. This book is just one of the many goals on my list. So, every day I work towards achieving these goals, and the day will come that my ambition will drive me to leave the best employer I have ever had.

I said all of that just to say this. As employers, managers, and supervisors, you can work hard to do everything right. You can have great promotional opportunities, benefits, perks, compensation, and work environment and still lose good people. But that's okay. Some employees will have ambitions that lead to promotional positions within your organization. While others, like myself, will have ambitions that may pull them away.

The entrepreneurial spirit should be nurtured at all levels and not discouraged. How would anyone ever have a job if no one ever had a desire to start a company? You never know where the next innovative idea or strategic partnership for your organization may come from.

For all you ambitious people, don't give up. It's hard going to a job everyday knowing that it's not your ultimate goal. My mother used to tell me that "nothing that comes easy is worth having." If you have a good job but are not happy, not everyone will understand that. Honestly, it's not for them to understand. All that matters is that you understand. Keep doing what you have to do, until you can do what you want to do.